piano • vocal • guitar
feel good fun

feel good fun

ISBN 0-7935-7566-4

HAL•LEONARD® CORPORATION

7777 W. BLUEMOUND RD. P.O. BOX 13819 MILWAUKEE, WI 53213

D1294948

Visit Hal Leonard Online at
www.halleonard.com

feel good fun

contents

ABC

Words and Music by ALPHONSO MIZELL, FREDERICK PERREN,
DEKE RICHARDS and BERRY GORDY

A B C eas - y as 1 2 3 ah sim - ple as

Do Re Mi; A __ B C; 1 2 3; *ba - by,* you and me girl.

Come on, let me love you just a lit - tle bit; I'm gon - na teach you how to sing it out.

Com - a, com - a, come on let me show you what it's all a - bout.

Bass Vamp

BABY I NEED YOUR LOVIN'

Words and Music by BRIAN HOLLAND,
LAMONT DOZIER and EDDIE HOLLAND

10

Lonely nights ___ echo your name, _____ Oh, ___ some-times I

won-der ___ will I ev-er be the same? ___ Oh yeah!

When you see me smil-ing, you know ___ things ___ have got-ten worse. ___

An-y smile ___ you might see ___ has all ___ been re-hearsed. ___

BACK IN MY ARMS AGAIN

Words and Music by BRIAN HOLLAND,
LAMONT DOZIER and EDWARD HOLLAND

Additional Lyrics

3. How can Mary tell me what to do
When she lost her love so true;
And Flo, she don't know
'Cause the boy she loves is a Romeo.
I listened once to my friends' advice
But it's not gonna happen twice.
'Cause all the advice ever's gotten me
Was many long and sleepless nights. Oo!
I got him back in my arms again.
Right by my side.
I got him back in my arms again
So satisfied. (Fade)

BAND OF GOLD

Words and Music by EDYTHE WAYNE
and RONALD DUNBAR

BIG GIRLS DON'T CRY

Words and Music by BOB CREWE
and BOB GAUDIO

22

BRANDY
(You're a Fine Girl)

Words and Music by
ELLIOT LURIE

BILLY, DON'T BE A HERO

Words and Music by PETER CALLENDER
and MITCH MURRAY

CODA

I heard she threw that let - ter _____ a - way. _____

Repeat and Fade

BUILD ME UP, BUTTERCUP

Words and Music by TONY McCAULEY
and MICHAEL D'ABO

THE CANDY MAN
from WILLY WONKA AND THE CHOCOLATE FACTORY

Words and Music by LESLIE BRICUSSE
and ANTHONY NEWLEY

DAYDREAM BELIEVER
featured in the Television Series THE MONKEES

Words and Music by
JOHN STEWART

DON'T SLEEP IN THE SUBWAY

Words and Music by TONY HATCH
and JACKIE TRENT

Don't sleep in the sub-way dar-ling the night is long_ For-get your fool-ish pride

noth-ing's wrong_ now you're be - side_ me a - gain.

gain.

gain. _____

DO YOU BELIEVE IN MAGIC

Words and Music by
JOHN SEBASTIAN

Do you be - lieve in mag - ic, in a young girl's heart? How the
mu - sic can free her when - ev - er it starts. And it's mag - ic if the
mu - sic is groov - y, it makes you feel hap - py like an

DON'T PULL YOUR LOVE

Words and Music by DENNIS LAMBERT
and BRIAN POTTER

MCA music publishing

EASY COME, EASY GO

Words and Music by JACK KELLER
and DIANE HILDERBRAND

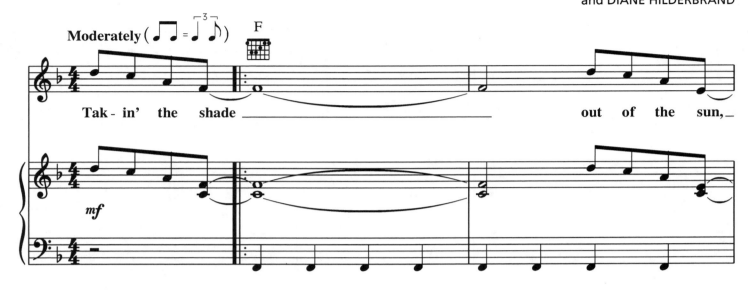

Tak-in' the shade _____ out of the sun, _____

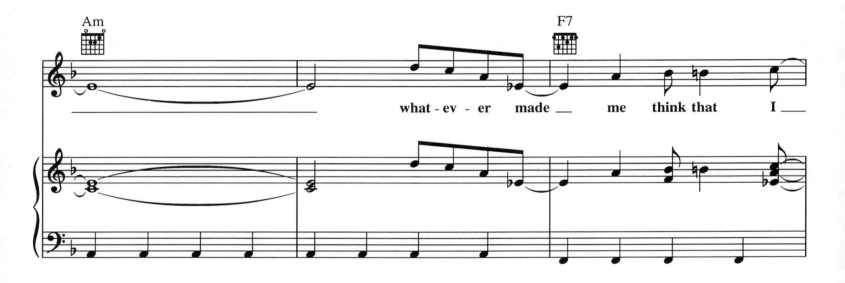

_____ what-ev-er made _ me think that I _

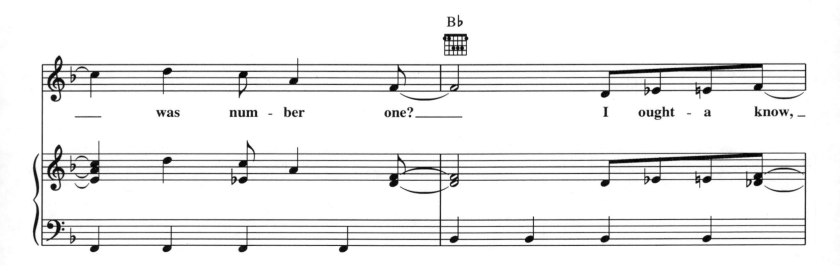

_ was num-ber one? _____ I ought-a know,

GEORGY GIRL

Words by JIM DALE
Music by TOM SPRINGFIELD

GIVE ME JUST A LITTLE MORE TIME

Words and Music by EDYTHE WAYNE
and RONALD DUNBAR

HOOKED ON A FEELING

Words and Music by
MARK JAMES

HANG ON SLOOPY

Words and Music by WES FARRELL
and BERT RUSSELL

HAPPY DAYS

Theme from the Paramount Television Series HAPPY DAYS

Words by NORMAN GIMBEL
Music by CHARLES FOX

HUNGRY

Words and Music by BARRY MANN
and CYNTHIA WEIL

I THINK I LOVE YOU
featured in the Television Series THE PARTRIDGE FAMILY

Words and Music by
TONY ROMEO

wor-ries me to say __ that I'd nev - er felt __ this way.

I'M HENRY VIII, I AM

Words and Music by FRED MURRAY
and R.P. WESTON

I WOKE UP IN LOVE THIS MORNING

Words and Music by IRWIN LEVINE
and LAWRENCE RUSSELL BROWN

but for my whole life through. _____

Oh, I ___ woke up in love ___ this morn - in'.

I ___ woke up in love ___ this morn - in'. Went to sleep with you ___

Repeat and Fade

___ on my mind. ___

Oh,

KICKS

Words and Music by BARRY MANN
and CYNTHIA WEIL

Girl, you thought you found the an - swer on that
think you're gon - na find your - self a

mag - ic car - pet ride last night.
lit - tle piece of par - a - dise.

But when you wake up in the morn - in', the world
But it ain't hap - pened yet, so girl,

KNOCK THREE TIMES

Words and Music by IRWIN LEVINE
and L. RUSSELL BROWN

LET'S HANG ON

Words and Music by BOB CREWE,
SANDY LINZER and DENNY RANDELL

Additional Lyrics

2. There isn't anything I wouldn't do.
    I'd pay any price to get in good with you.
    Patch it up. (Give me a second turnin'.)
    Patch it up. (Don't cool off while I'm burnin'.)

    You've got me cryin', dyin' at your door.
    Don't shut me out, ooh, let me in once more.
    Open up. (Your arms, I need to hold you.)
    Open up. (Your heart, oh girl, I love you.)

    Baby, don't you know?
    Baby, don't you go.
    Think it over and stay.

LIGHTNIN' STRIKES

Words and Music by LOU CHRISTIE
and TWYLA HERBERT

THE LITTLE OLD LADY

(From Pasadena)

Words and Music by DON ALTFELD
and ROGER CHRISTIAN

THE LOVE YOU SAVE

Words and Music by BERRY GORDY, ALPHONSO MIZELL,
FREDDIE PERREN and DENNIS LUSSIER

A LOVER'S CONCERTO

Words and Music by SANDY LINZER
and DENNY RANDELL

us, just to fall in love. You'll hold me in your

arms and say once a-gain you

love me. And if your love is true ev-'ry-thing will

Repeat and Fade

be just as won-der-ful.

MAKING OUR DREAMS COME TRUE

Theme from the Paramount Television Series LAVERNE AND SHIRLEY

Words by NORMAN GIMBEL
Music by CHARLES FOX

123

ME AND YOU AND A DOG NAMED BOO

Words and Music by
LOBO

MORE TODAY THAN YESTERDAY

Words and Music by
PAT UPTON

133

MIDNIGHT CONFESSIONS

Words and Music by
LOU JOSIE

MCA music publishing

135

ONE, TWO, THREE

Words and Music by JOHN MADARA,
DAVID WHITE and LEONARD BORISOFF

MCA music publishing

(I'm Not Your)
STEPPIN' STONE

Words and Music by TOMMY BOYCE
and BOBBY HART

140

SUGAR, SUGAR

Words and Music by ANDY KIM
and JEFF BARRY

THIS DIAMOND RING

Words and Music by AL KOOPER,
IRWIN LEVINE and BOB BRASS

Who wants to buy ____ this dia-mond ring? ____
This stone is gen-u-ine like love should be. ____

She took it off her fing-er, now it does-n't mean a
And if your ba-by's tru-er than my ba-by was to

THIS MAGIC MOMENT

Words and Music by DOC POMUS
and MORT SHUMAN

151

TIME WON'T LET ME

Words and Music by CHET KELLY
and TOM KING

Two Divided By Love

Words and Music by DENNIS LAMBERT,
BRIAN POTTER and MARTY KUPPS

WALK AWAY RENEE

Words and Music by MIKE BROWN,
TONY SANSONE and BOB CALILLI